DEVELOPING

THE
PROPHETIC
MINISTRY

DEVELOPING

THE PROPHETIC MINISTRY

BY FRANK DAMAZIO

Published by City Bible Publishing
9200 NE Fremont
Portland, Oregon 97220

Printed in U.S.A.

City Bible Publishing is a ministry of City Bible Church and is dedicated to
serving the local church and its leaders through the production and distribution
of quality materials.

It is our prayer that these materials, proven in the context of the local church,
will equip leaders in exalting the Lord and extending His kingdom.

*For a free catalog of additional resources from City Bible Publishing please
call 1-800-777-6057 or visit our web site at www.citybiblepublishing.com.*

ISBN 0-914936-85-9

Unless otherwise noted, all Scripture quotations are taken from the
King James version of the Bible. In some Scripture quotations italics
have been added by the author for emphasis.

Dedication

I would like to dedicate this book to *Pastor Leonard Fox*, who has served the Lord as a *prophet* to the Body of Christ for more than forty years, and whose example and preaching have encouraged and nurtured my love for the prophetic ministry.

Contents

Preface

The purpose of this book is to give an overview of the ministry of the prophets in the Old and New Testaments, and some practical guidelines for developing the prophetic ministry, in both its gifts and office in the Church today.

I have dealt more with the gift of prophecy than the office of a prophet, and have purposed this material to be used as a guideline on how to develop, nurture and maintain the practical verbal communication of the Holy Spirit to Christ's Body . . . the Church. This oral communication, the gift of prophecy, is a valuable gift that our Lord has given His Church.

We, as the Church, must further develop this gift and are responsible to guard it from becoming perverted. For the Lord, Himself, has given us this gift for the edification, exhortation, and comfort of the entire Body.

Pastor Frank Damazio

1

"Your Sons and Your Daughters Shall Prophesy"

The Church is living in a most exciting time because the Lord is restoring to her the Power of the Holy Spirit. God is preparing the Church by building character qualities deep within her, so that in future days she will be able to wisely manifest the anointing of the Spirit in an even greater measure. As the Lord is pouring forth His Spirit (Joel 2:28; Acts 2:17), He is challenging the Church to not only pray and sing in the Spirit, but also to *walk* and *live* in the Spirit.

With such an outpouring, the Gifts of the Holy Spirit will be restored and operative. The Holy Spirit desires to give the same gifts to the Church today as He did to the early Church. First Corinthians 12:7 states, "The manifestation of the Spirit is given to *every man* to profit withal." The Scriptures contain many references to the fact that both male and female, young and old will prophesy in the last days.

Joel 2:28. And it shall come to pass afterward, that I will pour out my spirit upon all flesh; and your *sons* and your *daughters* shall prophesy . . . (see also Acts 2:17-19)

Joel 2:29. And also upon the *servants* and upon the *handmaids* in those days will I pour out my spirit.

Luke 2:36. And there was one *Anna*, a *prophetess*, the daughter of Phanuel, of the tribe of Aser . . .

Acts 21:8-9. . . . . house of Philip the evangelist, which was one of the seven; and abode with him. And the same man had four *daughters*, virgins, which did prophesy.

I Corinthians 11:5. But every *woman* that *prayeth* or *prophesieth* . . .

This manifestation (or "shining forth") of the Spirit will be (in different degrees) part of every Christian's life, so the power of the Spirit that was operative in the early Church might be operative among her members again today.

Some Christians do not believe in the operation of the supernatural gifts of God as stated in I Corinthians 12:7-11. One reason for this is that they do not want to repeat the mistakes or extremes that "Spirit-filled" people have made (and are making) in the operation of the gifts. Although there have been abuses, counterfeits, and mistakes made in the functioning of the gifts, this does not invalidate the gifts themselves. Moreover, the gifts of the Holy Spirit are not only Scriptural, they were operative in the life of Jesus, in the early Church, and throughout Church history.

This generation is fortunate to be receiving the restoration of the gifts of the Holy Spirit. Those who desire to enter into the many blessings which the Holy Spirit holds for them will learn to follow the Scriptural guidelines for the gifts' operations.

One of the gifts of the Spirit which is receiving attention is the prophetic ministry. The purpose of this book is to give an overview of the ministry of the prophets in the Old and New Testaments, and some practical guidelines for developing the prophetic ministry, in both its gifts and office, in the Church today.

The Definition of the Word "Prophecy"

The word "prophecy" in Hebrew is *naba* which means "to flow, boil up or over; bubble or pour forth words, to gush" (Exodus 7:1-2; Proverbs 15:28). The Old Testament word for "prophet" means "a spokesman or speaker who is a special agent to deliver a message."

In the New Testament the words prophecy, prophesy, prophesied, and prophets are used approximately 186 times and mean "to speak, say; declare or make known." Thus the subject is given an important place in the New Testament for the Church.

When men would prophesy, whether in the Old or New Testament, the Spirit of God would inspire their speech and cause His own words to bubble forth. The same is true in the Church today. Men and women can utter words from the Lord as He inspires them to speak, for the edification, exhortation, and comfort of the entire Body.

2

The Four Realms of Prophecy

There are basically four realms of prophecy:

1. *Prophecy of Scripture*

All Biblical revelation prophesied through the Old and New Testament prophets is the *prophecy of Scripture*.

II Peter 1:20-21. Knowing this first, that no *prophecy of the scripture* is of any private interpretation. For the *prophecy* came not in old time by the will of man: but holy men of God spake as they were moved by the Holy Ghost.

The prophecy of Scripture speaks of the declaratory and revelatory elements of the Word of God as the highest revelation of God to man.

All prophetic utterance must be judged by the prophecy of Scripture. It contains no errors, mistakes, or imperfection. The written words which were recorded by the prophets and the apostles were supernaturally given by the inspiration of the Holy Spirit. Webster's Dictionary defines inspiration as "the supernatural influence of the Spirit of God on the human mind, by which the apostles and prophets and sacred writers were qualified to set forth divine truth without any mixture of error."

The prophecy of Scripture is the only kind of prophecy that can claim this level of inspiration. All other prophecy should be inspired by God but will not be direct revelation.

We must hold the logos, i.e., the written Word of God, as the highest and purest form of communication from God. However this does not substantiate the view which refuses to accept the oral communication of the gift of prophecy today. The Church needs both God's written Word and the prophetic word to grow in balance unto perfection.

2. *Spirit of Prophecy*

The second realm of prophecy in Scripture is the *spirit of prophecy*.

Revelation 19:10. And I fell at his feet to worship him. And he said unto me, See thou do it not: I am thy fellowservant, of thy brethren that have the testimony of Jesus: worship God: for the testimony of Jesus is the *spirit of prophecy*. (see also I Samuel 19:10; John 11:51)

The spirit of prophecy is the anointing of the Holy Spirit that enables men or women who do not have the gifts of prophecy or the office of a prophet to speak forth under the inspiration of God. Such an unction sometimes releases such a powerful presence of God in church services that almost anyone could "pick up" on the mind of the Lord for that occasion and declare it plainly. Yet just because a person speaks forth under the inspiration of the Spirit when a spirit of prophecy is present in a meeting does not mean that the person has the gift of prophecy or the mantle of a prophet.

3. *Gift of Prophecy*

The third realm of prophecy found in Scripture is the *gift of prophecy*.

I Corinthians 12:4. Now there are diversities of *gifts*, but the same Spirit.

I Corinthians 12:10. To another the working of miracles; to another prophecy . . . (see also I Corinthians 14:1, 3, 6)

The gift of prophecy is given to certain believers to bring the word of the Lord to the congregation. The revelation of the Lord is brought by the Holy Spirit to teach, encourage, and comfort the Body, or to exalt and crown the worship of Christ. Through this gift the living fire of Pentecost descends to believers to enflame and enkindle their spirits.

Not all Christians have the gift of prophecy, nor are preachers or pastors the only ones with such a gift, nor are all preachers and pastors necessarily anointed with the gift. The gift of prophecy is not the same as the ministry of preaching.

First, in the New Testament the prophetic gift and the ministry of preaching are used for different purposes. Second, the Greek words for prophecy and for preaching have different meanings:

Preaching. The Greek word for preaching is *enaggelizo*, which means "to announce good news, to declare a particular message of good tidings." This Greek word is used in I Corinthians 9:16, "For though I preach the *gospel*, I have nothing to glory of: for necessity is laid upon me; yea woe is unto me, if I preach not the gospel!"

Prophesying. The Greek word for prophesying is *propheteia, propheteuo*, which means "to predict something, to foretell events, or to speak under divine inspiration."

Prophesy. The Septuagint translators understood the Hebrew word *nabhi* (which was the Hebrew word used for prophesy) to mean "speaking for another, on behalf of another." In Greek this word is *prophetes*, a noun derived from the preposition *pro*, and the verb *phemi*, which is "to speak for another." This Greek word, accoring to *Thayer's New English Lexicon*, means "to utter forth, declare a thing which can only be known by divine revelation, to break forth under sudden impulse in lofty discourse or in praise of divine counsels."

Obviously the two words are not only different in meaning but also in their function under the anointing of the Holy Spirit. Certain churches have equated the gift of prophecy with the ministry of preaching because they no longer believed in or functioned in the realm of prophecy but still wanted to claim that their preachers had the same "authority" as prophetic utterances and prophets.

Those with the gift of prophecy should not be encouraged to move prophetically outside of their realm of edification, exhortation, and comfort.

4. *Office of Prophet*

The prophetic realm of foretelling and confirmation of ministries in the presbytery with the laying on of hands should only be done by those who have the mantle of the *office of prophet*, the fourth realm of prophecy.

Ephesians 2:19-20. Now therefore ye are no more strangers and foreigners, but fellowcitizens with the saints, and of the household of God; And are built upon the foundation of the apostles and prophets, Jesus Christ himself being the chief corner stone.

Ephesians 4:11. And he gave some, apostles; and some, *prophets*; and some, evangelists; and some, pastors and teachers. (see also Acts 13:1; 21:10ff; I Corinthians 12:28, 29)

Prophets are vessels whom Christ chooses to function constantly and accurately in the realm of the word of knowledge, word of wisdom, discernment of spirits, confirmation, revelation, illumination, prophetic utterance, prediction, visions, correction, and ministry confirmation.

Not all who prophesy are prophets. Paul clearly states that certain men are called to be prophets by the Lord and function in that ministry office to the Body of Christ. In the New Testament Church at Antioch, men such as Agabus were considered to be prophets of God. Just as Agabus moved in the realm of prediction (Acts 21: 10ff) and other New Testament prophets moved in the realm of presbytery confirmation of ministry (Acts 13:1ff), so will the prophets of today.

All of a prophet's utterances must be according to the Word of God. A prophet's revelation could not be accepted if it were to contradict the words of Jesus Christ or the Apostles. "If any man think himself to be a *prophet*, or spiritual, let him acknowledge that the things that I write unto you are the commandments of the Lord" (I Corinthians 14:37).

A prophet as a man is liable to error and thus his prophecy may contain error. The Lord admonishes us to judge and evaluate the prophet's word by the standard of Scripture and by the witness of the Spirit in the hearts of the believers. At the same time, the Spirit quickens the Word of Scripture or the hearts of other believers to confirm the truth of the prophet's word.

3

Prophetic Ministry in the Old and New Testaments

Prophecy is recorded in the Bible from the very beginning of time. Even before God prophesied about the hatred that would exist between the seed of the serpent and the seed of the woman (Genesis 3:15), Adam prophesied concerning marriage (Genesis 2:23, 24). Jesus used a man as far back in Bible history as Abel as a reference point after which the blood of all the slain prophets up to Zachariah would be required of Christ's unbelieving generation (Luke 11:49-51).

Enoch (Jude 14), Noah (Genesis 9:25-27; Hebrews 11:7), Jacob (Genesis 48, 49), and Joseph (Genesis 50:24; Hebrews 11:22) moved in degrees of prophecy. The Nazarites (Numbers 6:1ff; Amos 2:11,12) and the Rechabites (I Chronicles 2:55; II Kings 10:1-28; Jeremiah 35:6-10) were wholly separated unto God so that He could raise them up as His prophets. These men and every Old Testament prophet were forerunners who pointed to the Pattern Prophet, the Lord Jesus Christ.

Moses (Numbers 12:6; Deuteronomy 34:10) and Samuel (I Samuel 10:5; Acts 3:23-26; 13:20; Hebrews 11:32) are especially referred to as significant prophets in the Scriptures. For example, in Jeremiah 15:1 the Lord declares, "Even if Moses and Samuel were to stand before me, my heart would not go out to this people. Send them away from my presence! Let them go!" (NIV). Here the Lord pronounced to Jeremiah the prophet that even the interceding of Moses (the mediator of the Law) and Samuel (the founder of the schools of the prophets) would not curtail His wrath upon Israel.

Appeasement could come only from God sending His Son, Jesus, as the Pattern Intercessor, Prophet, and Priest to make reconciliation for Israel and the world. Jesus Christ would not only be the Pattern Priest who would teach the people the letter of the Law, but He would also be the Pattern Prophet (Deuteronomy 18:15-19) who would fulfill and demonstrate the very spirit of the Law.

Similarly, the ministry of the prophets in the Old Testament was always to show the true spiritual meaning behind the strict letter of the Law. Jesus did this by His very life and ministry. As God's last and final mouthpiece, the ultimate fulfillment of the Law, and prophet of the Judgment, Jesus Christ can be described as the One greater than the prophets (Hebrews 1:1-3).

In the New Testament, the ministry of the prophet is submitted to the ministry of the apostle (I Corinthians 12:28, 29) even though it is still a valid Ascension-gift ministry given to the Church by Jesus Christ (Ephesians 4:11). The prophetic office is under the apostolic office in the New Testament Church because all functioning of the prophetic office must be based on the historical facts and teachings of Jesus Christ recorded by the Apostles (Ephesians 2:20; 3:4-5).

Specifically, John the Baptist stands at the close of the realm of the supremacy of the prophetic ministry and at the opening of the realm of Christ's apostles. There is no record that Jesus chose any prophet before His Crucifixion and Ascension. This fact helps to confirm the submission of the prophetic office to the apostolic office in the Church Age.

Although the office of the prophet was, in a sense, on a somewhat higher level in the Old Testament than in the New Testament, there are still many similarities between their titles and functions. The following chart illustrates some of the differences and similarities between the prophets of the Old and New Testaments.

Old Testament Prophet	New Testament Prophet
1. Titles	**1. Titles**
a. seer	a. prophet
b. man of God	b. man of God
c. servant of the Lord	c. servant of the Lord
d. messenger of the Lord	d. messenger of the Lord
2. Function	**2. Function**
a. be a spokesman	a. be a spokesman, mouthpiece (Acts 13:1-2)
b. forthtell	b. forthtell (I Corinthians 14:8)
c. foretell	c. foretell - Agabus (Acts 11:27-28; Acts 21:10-11)
d. give guidance	d. no New Testament prophet was ever used in the controlling, guiding, or governing of a believer in the will of God; he was only used for confirmation
e. utter, write infallible Scripture	e. no new Testament prophet was ever used in the utterance or writing of infallible Scripture
f. pronounce judgment	f. pronounce judgment
g. be an interpreter of the Law	g. be an interpreter of the Law
h. admonish and reprove	h. minister the Word, exhortation, confirmation (Acts 15:32)
i. denounce prevailing sins	i. confirm Churches (Acts 15:32,41)
j. threaten people with terror of judgment	
k. call nations to repentance for idolatry; unfaithfulness; iniquity; social, moral, political corruption (Isaiah 58:1; 40:1-2; Malachi 4:4)	

Old Testament Prophet	New Testament Prophet
l. be a watchman standing upon the walls of Zion to sound the trumpet (Ezekiel 3:17; 33:7)	

3. The different kinds of prophets	**3. The different kinds of prophets**
a. prophets of guidance (Moses, Samuel)	a. prophets of confirmation
b. prophets of vision (Daniel, Zechariah)	b. prophets of vision (the Apostle John's revelation is connected to the prophet Daniel's)
c. prophets of Scripture (Isaiah)	c. prophets of Scripture (Pauline Epistles have prophetic implacability)
d. prophets of judgment	d. prophets of judgment

4. The different ways of communication	**4. The different ways of communication**
a. vision (Isaiah 1:1; Amos 8:1)	a. same as the Old Testament prophet
b. word (Jeremiah 2:1)	
c. dreams (Daniel 2:17)	
d. dark sayings	
e. words which he saw (Amos 1:1)	
f. burden (Nahum 1:1; Habakkuk 1:1)	
g. burning fire inside (Jeremiah 20:9)	

5. Prophet communicates the message to people in their basic way of understanding	**5. Prophet communicates the message to people in their basic way of understanding**
a. orally (Nathan to David)	a. same as Old Testament prophet
b. written word (books)	
c. symbolic acts (Isaiah walked naked; Hosea married harlot)	

4

The Prophetic Communication

God communicated with the prophets in different ways. Many times the means of communication and the ecstasy of the prophets caused others to call them "madmen" (II Kings 9:11; Hosea 9:7; Jeremiah 29:26) or "fools" (Hosea 9:7). The following are some of the ways that God's Spirit communicated to these men:

1. "The Word of the Lord came unto me"

2. "Thus saith the Lord"

3. "Hear the Word of the Lord"

4. "And the Spirit entered unto me when he spake unto me"

5. "The Lord spake unto me"

6. "The Word of the Lord that came to Hosea"

7. The Spirit entering into him (Ezekiel 2:2; 3:24)

8. The Spirit lifting him up and conveying him by vision to Jerusalem (Ezekiel 8:3; 11:1)

9. The hand of the Lord being upon them (Ezekiel 3:14; 37:1)

10. Daniel's visions, the effect they had on him (Daniel 8:15-18; 10:7-10)

11. The Spirit coming on them (Ezekiel 11:5; I Chronicles 12:48; II Chronicles 24:20; Isaiah 11:2; 61:1; II Peter 1:21)

5

The Symbolic Acts of the Prophets

The following are instances in which a prophet of God performed an action that represented a spiritual truth to the hearers:

1. Jeremiah wore a yoke around his neck through the streets to depict the impending Babylonian bondage (Jeremiah 27-28)

2. Hosea was commanded to marry a harlot, symbolizing Israel's unfaithfulness (Hosea 1-3)

3. Isaiah walked naked and barefoot for three years, symbolizing that Egypt and Ethiopia were at the hands of Assyria (Isaiah 20:1-6)

4. Ezekiel was commanded to lay mock siege to Jerusalem by portraying it upon a tile (Ezekiel 4:1-3)

5. Ezekiel was commanded to lie upon his left side for 390 days and upon his right side for 40 days. The number of days represented the number of years that Israel had disobeyed and forsaken God throughout their history (Ezekiel 4:4-8)

6. Ezekiel was commanded to eat different kinds of food for 390 days, symbolizing the ceremonial defilement that would come to the Israelites in being forced to partake of Gentile food during their captivity (Ezekiel 4:9-17)

7. Ezekiel was commanded to burn a portion of his hair, foretelling the coming destruction of Jerusalem and its inhabitants (Ezekiel 5:1-4)

8. Ezekiel was commanded to shave his hair and beard and scatter some of the hair, symbolizing the

scattering of a portion of the Jews to various parts of the earth (Ezekiel 5:1-4)

9. Ezekiel was commanded to prophesy to a dry bone yard, symbolizing Israel's spiritual dryness and death. This prophecy foretells the promised blessing upon Israel in and through the New Covenant (Ezekiel 37)

10. Ahizah, upon meeting Jeroboam, rent his garment in twelve pieces, symbolizing the division of his kingdom (II Kings 11:30)

11. Jeremiah symbolically gave signs to Israel by:
a. a marred girdle (symbolizing the negative effect the seventy-year captivity in Babylon would have upon the house of Judah; Jeremiah 13:1)
b. a potter and the clay (speaking of the judgment of God coming to the house of Judah and the resulting blessing upon them in and through the New Covenant; Jeremiah 18:1)
c. a cup of the wine of wrath (speaking of the judgment of God being stored up for ungodly nations; Jeremiah 25:15)

12. Certain prophets were commanded to give prophetic, symbolic names to their children:
a. Isaiah's children —
Shear-jashub: "A remnant shall return" (Isaiah 7:3)
Maher-shalah-hash-baz: "The spoil speedeth, the prey hasteth" (Isaiah 8:1)

b. Hosea's children —
Jezreel: "It will be sown of God"
Lo-Ruhamah: "No mercy"
Lo-Ammi: "Not my people"

13. Ezekiel was commanded to prophesy to the mountains. Mountains in Scripture represent various kingdoms and nations of the earth (Ezekiel 6:1-3)

14. Ezekiel was commanded to move by digging through a wall, representing Judah's being removed to Babylon (Ezekiel 12:1-6)

15. Jeremiah was commanded to buy a linen girdle, to put it on but not wash it, and then to go to the Euphrates and hide it there in a hole of the rock. Then he was commanded to dig it up, even though it was marred and good for nothing, symbolizing what God was going to do to the pride of Jerusalem and Judah (Jeremiah 13:1-11)

16. Jeremiah was commanded to take an earthen vessel in front of the ancients of the people and the ancients of the priests, symbolizing the destruction of Jerusalem (Jeremiah 19:1-9)

17. Ezekiel remained dumb for seven days after his call, representing his identification with the miseries and trials of those to whom he would minister (Ezekiel 3:15)

18. Agabus bound the Apostle Paul with his girdle, symbolizing what the Jews were going to do to him in Jerusalem (Acts 21:10-14)

Symbolic acts in the prophetic ministry are still valid today. Several years ago in southern California I knew of a prophet who, upon the quickening of the Holy Spirit, cut the pastor's tie in 40 pieces and declared that $40,000 would come into the church by a certain date. This obviously surprised some people, and even offended some, but the money did come in before the date the prophet had given. All were in awe regarding the greatness of God. I do not suggest that a person take such abnormal measures in communicating the words of God unless directly inspired by God.

6

Developing the Ministry of Prophecy

I Corinthians 12:31. But covet earnestly the *best* gifts . . .

I Corinthians 13:9. For we *know* in *part,* and we prophesy in part.

I Corinthians 14:3. But he that *prophesieth* speaketh unto men to *edification,* and *exhortation,* and *comfort.*

I Corinthians 14:4. He that speaketh in an unknown tongue edifieth himself; but he that *prophesieth edifieth* the *church.*

Many leaders and Christians wonder how to develop the prophetic ministry. It is the Lord who must sovereignly anoint, equip, and use a person in any realm of prophecy. Yet He wants us to earnestly desire and aspire to the spiritual gifts. There are some basic guidelines which can be followed to prepare for and to develop the prophetic gift.

1. *Realize that prophecy was a vital part of the early Church ministry.*

Therefore prophecy is to be a vital part of the present day New Testament Church (Joel 2:28-29; Luke 2:36; Acts 2:16-19; 19:6; 21:9; I Corinthians 11:5; I Thessalonians 5:20).

Prophecy brings the fire of Pentecost to the church meetings. Prophecy comes from the Spirit, whereas preaching comes from the intellect. The preacher's training and skill are touched by the Spirit to bring the teaching of the gospel to the meeting. The difference between prophecy and preaching must be clearly seen. Otherwise, the New Testament understanding of prophecy will not be practiced, and there will not be enough faith to operate in this realm of the supernatural.

2. *Release the faith to prophesy.*

Faith is important for prophecy because one can only speak forth in this way according to the proportion of his faith (Romans 12:6-8). Faith is a gift from God, but it is like a mustard seed planted in each person's life that needs to grow every day.

To increase one's faith for this realm one must constantly hear and study the Word of God (and not the word of the devil) because only through the Word does faith arise (Romans 10:8-10,17). With a dynamic prayer and Word life depositing the seed of the Word within his heart, a Christian is in a good position to have God quicken that Word and to cause faith to arise to prophesy what the Lord has given. The greater the faith (not the presumption) of a Christian, the greater his depth of prophecy.

3. *Learn to operate and flow in the anointing of the Holy Spirit.*

Being filled with the Holy Spirit is the all important condition to bring forth the words of the Lord. The spiritual gift is given forth in the Spirit's anointing. The unction of the Holy Spirit cannot be seen in human terms of ability. It is God's own enabling power operating through a humble vessel. The Holy Spirit takes the deep things of God and anoints the prophet to give them forth to the people.

All of God's prophets were anointed to take on the mantle of a prophet and be used of God. (Elijah: I Kings 19:15, 16; David: I Samuel 16:12, 13; Jesus Christ: Isaiah 61:1; Psalm 45:6, 7; Messiah means "Anointed One").

To increase the anointing of the Spirit in a person's life, one must be a yielded channel through whom He can flow. One must be broken by God, for it is only the broken, contrite heart that God can trust with His gifts. A Christian, too, must receive the Baptism of the Holy Spirit (accompanied by speaking in tongues) and have a deep life of obedience and communion with God. As a believer yields his life to the Lord and listens to the inner voice of the Holy Spirit, he will grow in flowing in the anointing of the Holy Spirit. He will be more sensitive to follow the anointing of the Spirit when he prophesies the word of God.

4. Learn how to receive a word from the Lord.

Proverbs 4:4 declares, "Let thine heart retain my words . . ." The Spirit will give a word to a person by means of a single word (e.g., "unity"), a sentence (e.g., "Thou shall love one another . . ."), a spiritual burden, a vision, or a spiritual thought that gives a quickening of joy to the person at the time.

Jeremiah 15:16. Thy word was unto me the joy and rejoicing of mine heart . . .

Jeremiah 20:9. But His word was in mine heart as a burning fire shut up in my bones . . .

A word of prophesy comes as a word of joy and burning to a person's heart before he gives it. A word of prophecy is not just a passing good thought or idea. It is a quickened, Spirit-anointed burden and word from the Lord that gives its recipient a definite feeling of the need for its expression (Psalm 119:11, 16, 25, 50, 148).

The word that the Lord gives should always edify (build up), exhort (encourage), or comfort (bring consolation and a refreshing to) the people of God (I Corinthians 14:3).

5. Move out at the right time in the meeting.

It is taken for granted here that the house of the Lord is the Biblical and safe setting for the functioning of the spiritual gifts. (Notice how many times the word "Church," or a word with the same meaning, is mentioned in the main New Testament chapter concerning the operation of the spiritual gifts: I Corinthians 14:4, 5, 6, 12, 16, 19, 23, 26, 28, 33, 34, 35).

Prophesying "at any old time" in a church meeting is not appropriate. One must interject his prophesy at a time that would be most edifying for all involved. The Holy Spirit expresses different moods in different meetings, and the Christian who believes that he has a prophetic word for the church must ask himself, "What is the mood of the Spirit in this meeting?"

It is possible that the word the person has received from the Lord is only for himself or for a later time. These things must be properly discerned in every meeting by the person who believes that he has a prophetic word. To prophesy during the offering, the announcements, the singing, or when someone else is speaking would be obviously unedifying and therefore out of order. A good way to learn how to move out at the right time is to observe when the more mature and seasoned prophetic ministries operate.

6. *Learn to discern one's own thoughts and feelings from those of the Holy Spirit.*

It is very important that a person does not project his preconceived thoughts and ideas into the prophetic stream. However, this caution is not to put new ministries into such a bondage of fear that they do not have the liberty to function. A person learns to prophesy as a child learns to walk. It takes a number of falls before he can walk steadily by himself.

If a person is going through some specific problem or emotional anxiety, he may have a tendency to prophesy these things. For example, if a person were being moved upon by the Holy Spirit to forgive someone and the person had not yet done this, he might project what the Spirit was saying to him upon the congregation with the words: "Thus saith the Lord to this people, 'Thou shalt learn better to forgive one another. For, surely, the Lord is calling you to a greater level of forgiveness.' " In doing this, the person may be putting his own thoughts, dealings, needs, problems, and questions onto the congregation.

This is unanointed, unedifying, and unfortunate for the people because they can be sidetracked from what the Spirit wanted to say to them. The Old Testament refers to men that do this as false prophets who "prophesy out of their own heart and visions."

One must remember that even in a church meeting one's thoughts can come from different sources — God, oneself, or the devil. It is not beyond a Spirit-filled Christian to speak the wrong words; we are human and liable to error. For example, Jesus had to rebuke Peter, the great Apostle to the Jews, for allowing Satan to speak through his mouth (Matthew 16:23). If this can happen to Peter, it can happen to a Christian today.

In order to make one's heart and mind more accessible to the Spirit, a Christian must cleanse and transform his mind daily through the Word of God (Romans 12:1-3). He must learn how to bring every thought into obedience to Jesus Christ (II Corinthians 10:1-6). Having a clean heart and a transformed mind will allow the Holy Spirit to more easily bring forth a clear, spiritual word of prophecy.

7. Stir up your gift.

In the Greek the word "stir" means to "rekindle; to stir the coals that are almost out." Because spiritual gifts can be quenched through sin, neglect, and laziness, many times they must not only be rekindled, but rekindled by the Spirit. The Bible speaks very clearly of the necessity of spiritual stirring. The following Scriptures illustrate this principle.

***

Exodus 35:21. Every one whose heart *stirred* him up . . . brought the Lord's offering to the work of the tabernacle.

Job 17:8. The innocent man shall stir up himself against the hypocrite.

27

Psalm 35:23. Stir up thyself . . . even unto my cause, my God and my Lord.

II Timothy 1:6. . . . stir up the gift of God, which is in thee by the putting on of my hands. (NIV) — For this reason I remind you to fan into flame the gift of God, which is in you through the laying on of my hands.

II Peter 3:1. . . . I *stir* up your pure minds by way of remembrance.

A person can stir himself spiritually through fasting, earnest prayer, and the reading aloud of God's Word. Spiritual stirring is very necessary for the operation of the prophetic mantle.

8. Cultivate a hunger for spiritual gifts.

Many Christians and many local churches do not function freely in spiritual gifts because they do not have a Godly desire to see them operate. Without an earnest thirst for the Spirit to operate the gifts in the Church, she will not see the manifestation of the power of God. It is as Jesus said, "According to your faith, be it unto you."

The word "covet" ("have a strong desire toward") is used twelve times in the New Testament and applies to the seeking of spiritual gifts. First Corinthians 12:31 states, "Covet earnestly the best gifts . . ." It is clear from these admonitions of Paul that God desires the Church to have a healthy hunger after spiritual gifts (cf. Acts 7:9; I Corinthians 11:2; 14:1; Galatians 4:17-18, where "covet" is translated in different ways).

Jesus said, "Blessed are they which do hunger and thirst after righteousness: for they shall be filled" (Matthew 5:6). The word "desire" means "to have warmth of feeling toward; to be zealous for."

Paul the Apostle uses the word "zealous" in I Corinthians 14:12: "Even so ye, forasmuch as ye are zealous of spiritual gifts, seek that ye may excel to the edifying of the church." The following scriptures show that God wants to grant His people their Godly desires for spiritual things, including spiritual gifts.

Psalm 21:2. Thou hast given him his heart's desire . . .

Psalm 37:4. . . . and he shall give thee the desires of thine heart.

Proverbs 11:23. The desire of the righteous is only good . . .

I Corinthians 14:1. . . . desire spiritual gifts, but rather that ye may prophesy.

---

9. Speak forth the Word of God for the purposes of God.

God intended His Word to accomplish many spiritual ends. In His descriptions of His Word are set forth His very purposes:

1. The Word as a fire which purifies from dross (Jeremiah 23:29)

2. The Word as a hammer which breaks bondages (Jeremiah 23:29)

3. The Word as a lamp which gives direction (Psalm 119:105)

4. The Word as a mirror which causes a person to see his real self (James 1:21-25)

5. The Word as milk which gives spiritual nourishment to spiritual babes (I Peter 2:2)

6. The Word as a rod which measures the Church (Revelation 11:1-2)

7. The Word as a seed which produces faith and growth (I Peter 1:23)

8. The Word as a sword which defends and discerns one's heart (Hebrews 4:12)

9. The Word as water which cleanses and refreshes the soul (Ephesians 5:26)

10. The Word as honey which tastes good to the soul (Psalm 19:7-10)

11. The Word as bread which feeds the soul and supplies one's spiritual needs (Matthew 4:4)

12. The Word as an ox goad which prods a person onward (Ecclesiastes 12:11)

Each one of these picture-words demonstrates a truth about the purpose of the prophetic word ministry for the Church. Furthermore, the prophetic word from the Lord is to be the word of:

13. Healing (Psalm 107:20)

14. Hope (Psalm 119:114, 147; 130:5)

15. Strength (Psalm 119:116)

16. Rejoicing (Psalm 119:162; Proverbs 12:25)

17. Deliverance (Psalm 119:170)

18. Proper timing (Proverbs 15:23)

19. Fruition (Isaiah 55:8-11)

20. Life (Philippians 2:16; I John 1:1)

21. Christ (Colossians 3:16)

22. Exhortation (Hebrews 13:22)

Believers who minister with the prophetic gift would do well to realize that these twenty-two descriptions of the Word of God should also be descriptive of the word of prophecy they bring forth.

10. Receive the quickening of the Holy Spirit.

The word translated "quickening" is used twelve times in the New Testament and means "to make alive" and "to give life." This word is translated in different ways. In I Corinthians 3:6 it is "giveth life" and in Galatians 3:21 it is "giving life."

A person who prophesies must learn how to be quickened in his own spirit by the Holy Spirit. The quickening of the Spirit is the very breath of this ministry. The written

Word of God was inspired ("God breathed") by the Spirit, and thus the prophetic word must be brought to life by the same Spirit.

The Spirit will give the thoughts of the Lord to the congregation, lifting the people to the spiritual realm and quickening them in body, mind, soul, and spirit.

The following Scriptures show the importance of the quickening of the Spirit:

Psalm 119:25, 154. *Quicken* thou me according to thy word.

Ephesians 2:1, 5. And you hath he *quickened*, who were dead in trespasses and sins.

I Peter 3:18. For Christ . . . being put to death in the flesh, but *quickened* by the Spirit.

John 6:63. It is the spirit that *quickeneth* . . .

I Timothy 6:13. . . . in the sight of God, who quickeneth all things.

A person who prophesies should prophesy only when he senses the inner prompting and quickening of the Spirit upon him. In this way he will be assured that his utterances are inspired by God, and that they will edify the congregation. Again, a life of prayer, obedience, worship, and reading the Word will kindle the Spirit's quickening power in a believer's life.

11. Be sensitive to the lifting of the prophetic spirit.

Before a Christian begins to prophesy he usually senses, to some degree, the anointing of God upon him. As he responds to this anointing and steps out by faith with a prophetic utterance, the Holy Spirit will increase His prophetic anointing. However, as soon as the Holy Spirit's message has been adequately communicated, the person prophesying will sense a lifting or lessening of the prophetic unction. At this time it is good for the person to be sensitive to the Spirit's leading and prepare to stop when the Spirit ceases to enable him to flow forth.

Some prophecies are long and some are short, but the important thing to remember is that one must start and stop according to the flow of the anointing.

12. Learn how to begin speaking in the prophetic spirit.

Getting started in a prophetic flow is possibly the most difficult part of moving in prophecy. Yet the more you do it, the easier it becomes. One's first step must be taken in boldness and faith. The word "bold" is used in the New Testament approximately sixteen times and includes the following ideas:

- to act with unexpected or seemingly extreme conduct
- to set out with a definite goal
- to venture forth
- to dare to do something
- to utter something unreservedly
- to lose all fear of something

When a person prophesies, he must lose all fear of himself, others, the possibility of mispronouncing words, missing the correct prophetic flow, prophesying uninspired words from the devil, being adjusted afterwards, and operating in a strange, unknown realm. When a person prophesies God's word, he must be totally God-conscious. This sensitivity to God's presence upon him will enable him to be bold in a gentle and humble way.

God desires His people to be bold in Him. The following Scriptures illustrate this:

Proverbs 28:1. The righteous are *bold* as a lion . . .

Acts 13:46. Paul and Barnabas waxed *bold* . . .

Philippians 1:14. And many of the brethren in the Lord . . . are much more *bold* to speak the word without fear.

Ephesians 6:19, 20. . . . that I may open my mouth *boldly* . . . that therein I may speak *boldly*, as I ought to speak.

A key to boldness is being filled with the holy fear of the Lord rather than with the natural fear of man. The following chart compares the two sources of fear.

The Fear of the Lord	*The Fear of Man*
1. Having therefore these promises, dearly beloved, let us cleanse ourselves from all filthiness of the flesh and spirit, perfecting holiness in the fear of God. (II Corinthians 7:1)	1. For ye have not received the spirit of bondage again to fear . . . (Romans 8:15)
2. For behold this self same thing, that ye sorrowed after a godly sort, what carefulness it wrought in you . . . what fear . . . and . . . zeal . . . ! (II Corinthians 7:11)	2. For God hath not given us the spirit of fear; but of power, and of love, and of a sound mind. (II Timothy 1:7)
3. Submitting yourselves one to another in the fear of God. (Ephesians 5:21)	3. So that we may boldly say, The Lord is my helper, and I will not fear what man shall do unto me. (Hebrews 13:6)
4. And many of the brethren in the Lord, waxing confident by my bonds, are much more bold to speak the word without fear. (Philippians 1:14)	4. There is no fear in love; but perfect love casteth out fear: because fear hath torment. He that feareth is not made perfect in love. (I John 4:18)

In Christ we can overcome our fears and learn to trust in the Spirit of God. To yield to timidity is to yield to the flesh. As with any spiritual ministry, the prophetic gift must be built by faith. If a member rises up to the quickening of the Holy Spirit, the Spirit will meet him with His anointing and bring forth what is needed.

13. Cultivate self-control and temperance in the operation of the prophetic gift.

Many times younger Christians will become so excited at sensing the anointing of God's Spirit upon them that they will tend to lose self-control and may even become fanatical in their expression of the prophetic flow. Christians who are just beginning in the flow of prophecy must be particularly careful that they do not become excessively excited when they are touched by God's Presence. The following verses admonish the Christian in this area:

Proverbs 25:28. He that hath *no rule* over his *own spirit* is like a city that is broken down, and without walls.

Proverbs 29:11. A fool uttereth all his mind but a wise man *keepeth* it in till afterwards.

Proverbs 29:20. Seest thou a man that is *hasty* in his words? there is more hope of a fool than of him.

Ecclesiastes 5:1,2. Keep thy foot when thou goest to the house of God, and be more ready to hear, than to give the sacrifice of fools: for they consider not that they do evil. Be not *rash* with thy *mouth*, and let not thine heart be *hasty* to utter any thing before God: for God is in heaven, and thou upon earth: therefore let thy words be few.

I Corinthians 14:32. And the spirits of the prophets are *subject* to the prophets.

When a person prophesies he must realize that he himself is in control of his expressions and emotions. God anoints, but He does not overpower. God moves, but He moves in a wise way. Every Christian who operates in the prophetic realm should learn to control his gift along with its expression. He should also learn to give place to the next person and prefer him in honor. When there is self-control and temperance in the ministry of the prophetic gifts, each local church can be greatly edified.

14. Be inwardly impressed to be a fervent worshipper.

When we worship from the heart, God meets with us and brings the anointing of His Presence (Psalm 22:3). God's anointing releases the operation of the spiritual gifts. A fruitful Christian will make singing, thanksgiving, praise, and worship a vital part of his daily life. When one rejoices with the Lord, his spirit becomes one with the Lord. Not only is the gift able to be stirred up, the heavenly realms are stirred up.

7

How to Channel the Prophetic Ministry

We not only need to stir and release the prophetic ministry, we also need to channel it properly to the Body. When a church is filled with the Spirit and the blessings of His gifts, there must be specific guidelines for their operation. There are always those who will misuse and abuse the freedom of the Spirit.

In the Old Testament, Samuel established a school of prophets, thus confirming the need for specific training in the realm of the prophetic. The following is a brief outline of some of the major facts concerning the sons (or schools) of the prophets which Samuel formed:

1. Their means of support (I Samuel 9:8; Numbers 22:7; II Kings 5:15; 8:8; I Kings 17:6)

2. Their dwellings (Bethel, Gilgal, Mizpah, Ramah — I Samuel 7:15-17; II Kings 2)

3. Some were married (II Kings 4:1-2)

4. Received spiritual instruction (II Kings 4:38; 6:1; I Samuel 19:20)

5. Prophesied together (Isaiah 10:5ff)

6. Were spiritual messengers (II Kings 9:1 — Elisha sent to anoint Jehu king; I Kings 20:35-43)

The School of the Prophets made teaching available to the younger prophets in training. This teaching was a combination of the Law of Moses, the history of Israel, the covenants given to the people of the Lord, and the practical principles of living as a prophet. Most of the younger prophets would be discipled by a veteran prophet for the impartation of truth through Godly example.

The prophetic ministry is not such that a person can receive the anointing to prophesy through teaching, but he can receive teachings on how to channel and operate the prophetic gift he possesses. Anyone desiring to function in the prophetic ministry, congregational prophecy, prophetic "song of the Lord," etc., needs to have these guidelines by which to carefully examine himself. The river of God's Spirit must remain pure and unpolluted by human pride, egotism, or other works of the flesh. It is possible to have the right attitudes and desires in our hearts, but the wrong practices when moving in the prophetic. Let us look at some main areas we must be careful of while desiring to move in the prophetic.

1. Are we ministering from the right motivations?

II Corinthians 13:5. Examine yourselves, whether ye be in the faith; prove your own selves. Know ye not your own selves . . .

The word motivation means "an inner drive that causes one to act in a certain way, an inner impulse." Everyone has motivations, some good, some bad. Because we are all born in and have an Adamic nature with its desires, carnal habits, and selfish motivations, we must be honest before the Lord and with ourselves in order to discern our true motivations. Why do we do the things we do? What force is driving us to do these things? Some of the questions we should ask ourselves are:

Do we move in the prophetic to prove our spirituality?

Do we move in the prophetic to be *seen by others* and receive *recognition* and *praise*?

Do we move in the prophetic to be like some man of God we admire and want to be identified with?

Do we move in the prophetic to establish our

ministry as a prophet and thus receive more authority and recognition?

Do we move in the prophetic because we want to prophesy to the whole church what God is speaking to our own hearts?

The Book of Proverbs is called the book of wisdom, or the book for right living. Let us examine our motivations by the light of its profound principles.

Proverbs 25:6. "Put not forth thyself in the presence of the king . . ." This Scripture speaks of pushing oneself forward to be seen or honored. The thought here is to avoid carnal ambition.

Proverbs 18:16. "A man's gift maketh room for him, and bringeth him before great men." If a person possesses a gift of God he need not be concerned about acceptance or recognition. The gift will cause people to open themselves to the ministry of the prophet. The motivation we must always examine is self-ambition. Am I bringing attention to myself and my gift, or do I rest in the principles of God?

Proverbs 17:19. "He that exalteth his gate seeketh destruction." In Scripture the gate was symbolic of a man's position in the city as one of the decision makers, leaders, or elders. The book of wisdom instructs us not to exalt our own leadership or ministry, because destruction of both gift and person will result (Proverbs 18:12).

The prophetic gift is not to be used by self-ambitious people to establish their own reputations. We should not be driven by our reputation, nor by the dictates of our Adamic nature. Rather we should gently yield to the quickening of the Holy Spirit.

2. Are we monopolizing the prophetic ministry in the corporate gatherings?

To monopolize means "to secure and retain exclusive possession or control of something, to take advantage of a privilege so as to have control." The prophetic ministry is for the Body of Christ to be edified and encouraged.

It is a spiritual privilege to minister unto the Church of God in this particular ministry. Most churches which have a strong prophetic flow also have a free flowing style of worship and response to the Lord. Within this kind of atmosphere where ministry to the Lord and to one another is encouraged, there is the possibility of people misusing or taking advantage of the openness in the meetings.

The leadership of the church is responsible for setting guidelines that will protect the river of God in the worship service. In every congregation there seem to be people who feel they are the mouthpiece of the Lord for *every* meeting. While we teach Body Ministry (the idea that each member has something to impart to the corporate gathering), still the church is bound by a few people who continually monopolize the meeting with their prophetic gift.

Taking advantage of the corporate gathering of God's people should be corrected by the local leadership. There must be a clear discernment between being moved by individual personality or by the anointing of God. Some people have an outgoing personality and have no fear of speaking in a public meeting, while others with a more self-conscious personality have great difficulty in speaking out. If the local leadership does not correct those who are monopolizing, the shy ones with a true word from God may never speak unto the Body of Christ. The pastor of the assembly would be wise to teach on distinguishing the quickening of the Spirit from the promptings of the emotions of the flesh.

There is also a difference between prophecy and exhortation. Some prophecies should be given as a short testimony or exhortation to the whole Body. The important principle for the church to establish is the principle of honoring and preferring one another in the Lord.

I Corinthians 12:26. And whether one member suffer, all the members suffer with it; or one member be honoured, all the members rejoice with it.

I Corinthians 14:30. If any thing be revealed to another that sitteth by, let the first hold his peace.

Romans 12:3-8. For I say, through the grace given unto me, to every man that is among you, not to think of himself more highly than he ought to think; but to think soberly, according as God hath dealt to every man the measure of faith.

For as we have many members in one body, and all members have not the same office:

So we, being many, are one body in Christ, and every one members one of another.

Having then gifts differing according to the grace that is given to us, whether prophecy, let us prophesy according to the proportion of faith;

Or ministry, let us wait on our ministering: or he that teacheth, on teaching;

Or he that exhorteth, on exhortation: he that giveth, let him do it with simplicity; he that ruleth, with diligence; he that sheweth mercy, with cheerfulness.

3. Are we allowing mixture in the prophetic ministry?

Revelation 22:1. And he shewed me a pure river . . .

The word "mixture" means "that which consists of different ingredients blended without order, that which contains two or more elements, that which is confused or muddled." Whenever we are moving in the gifts of the Holy Spirit there is the possibility of mixture. Mixture in the prophetic ministry means whatever would pollute the pure flow of the Holy Spirit in the prophetic word. This could arise from carnality, sensuality, hidden habits, personality weaknesses, wrong motivations, emotional stress — rough edges anywhere in our being.

Man is a triune being (I Thessalonians 5:23) made up of body, soul, and spirit. The Holy Spirit is made one with our spirit at the time of salvation (I Corinthians 6:17 — "But he that is joined unto the Lord is one spirit"). Mixture comes when we blend together the feelings and words of our soul with the words and anointing of the Holy Spirit. Mixture is something we must all deal with, for all Christians are imperfect, born in sin and shapen in iniquity. Paul says we prophesy in *part*, and we know in part (I Corinthians 13:9).

A believer may be influenced by a number of harmful external and internal forces which will consequently bring mixture into his prophetic ministry. Here are a few by example:

- The satanic spirit
- Limited personal concepts of God or people
- An incorrect doctrinal interpretation of Scripture
- Present pressures and circumstances
- The emotion of the public meeting
- Marital disagreement
- Human knowledge of a certain situation

The vessel who is to be used by the Lord must maintain his purity. It is our responsibility to keep our hearts, minds, and spirits clean and ready to respond to the Lord.

James 4:8. Purify your hearts, ye double minded.

I Corinthians 5:7. Purge out therefore the old leaven . . .

II Timothy 2:21. If a man therefore purge himself from these. . .

Hebrews 9:14. Purge your conscience . . .

Proverbs 4:23. Keep thy heart with all diligence . . .

4. Are we using "thus saith the Lord" with looseness?

I Samuel 3:19. And Samuel grew, and the Lord was with him, and did let none of his *words fall* to the *ground.*

Words are the vehicle by which we communicate our inner thoughts. When God chose to speak to man, He chose the vehicle of words. When God speaks, everyone should listen carefully and respect what has been spoken. When God commands, everyone should properly respond by obedience. When man speaks to man through oral communication, we should also hear, analyze, and respond accordingly. But when God speaks through man, we are obligated to respond as if God Himself were standing there speaking to us.

When God spoke to man in Old Testament times, the terms "Thus saith the Lord," or "This is the Lord speaking now" were used. The Hebrew word for God is translated "Yahweh." In the Hebrew nation this was a most sacred and holy name. They were not allowed to use this name in their everyday conversation unless it was used with great respect and honor. The Hebrews believed that once the name "Yahweh" was uttered, something *exciting* and *dynamic* would happen. The prophets were the appointed ministers to use this name with authority as they delivered "the Word of the Lord."

In many churches today, people often prophesy in the *name* of the Lord, using "thus saith the Lord" as their stamp of authority. One of the problems is that something less than dynamic seems to happen. Could it be that the term "thus saith the Lord" should be saved and used sparingly by the appointed prophets?

Isaiah 55:11. So shall my word be that goeth forth out of my mouth: it shall not return unto me void.

Isaiah 44:26. That confirmeth the *word* of His servant, and *performeth* the counsel of His messengers.

Jeremiah 1:9. I have put *my words* in thy mouth.

Exodus 4:12. Now therefore go, and I will be with thy *mouth*, and teach thee *what* thou shalt *say*.

8

What Not to Do When Moving in the Prophetic Word

When a person moves in the spiritual gifts, there are always areas in which he should be careful. There are certain principles that can be learned through wise counsel. The following is a list of guidelines that a person should be careful *not* to do when operating in the prophetic ministry. These are given in the context of a local church corporate gathering.

1. Speak so softly that no one can hear the word

2. Speak so swiftly that no one can understand the word

3. Speak so long that no one can remember the first part of the word

4. Speak the same word as the previous speaker: there is a difference in speaking confirmation and being redundant

5. Speak anything contrary to the flow of the Spirit

6. Speak harsh condemnation and judgment against the local church

7. Speak with distracting mannerisms that draw attention to themselves rather than to the word

8. Speak so many times that you monopolize the church meeting

9. Speak first, if you are a novice, rather than letting the more mature ministries set the flow of the meeting

10. Speak of yourself as being spiritual because of your manifestation of a gift; gifts do not indicate Christian maturity or spirituality (cf. I Corinthians 3:1-2 and 12:1ff)

9

Limitations of the Prophetic Ministry

I Corinthians 13:9. (AMP) For our knowledge is fragmentary, incomplete and imperfect, and our prophecy is fragmentary, incomplete and imperfect.

As stated earlier there are four levels of prophecy: the Prophecy of Scripture, the Office of the Prophet, the Gift of Prophecy, and the Spirit of Prophecy. Of these four realms, only the prophecy of Scripture — the written Word of God, our Bible — is without any error or limitation. The prophecy of Scripture is the measuring rod and judge of all other realms of prophecy.

If the spoken prophetic word does not agree with the written Word of God, we must not receive it. Prophecy given by man is never infallible, without error, and forbidden to question. If a prophet claims infallibility, we know that he is in error and dangerous to listen to. The office of the prophet, gift of prophecy, and spirit of prophecy are not without limitation, not without imperfection.

I have met people in strong Spirit-filled local churches who live by their personal prophecies. These prophecies could have been received in a home fellowship meeting, a local church Sunday service, or in special presbytery meetings. These people move their families, quit jobs or take jobs, marry, choose careers and ministries, interpret personal circumstances, explain certain decisions, make business investments — all based on a particular personal prophecy. They carry their prophecies in their Bible and quote sections from them as readily as they quote the Bible, and sometimes better! This creates a problem of imbalance and eventually will lead a person into a mild form of religious deception.

As Christians we are not allowed to exalt anything above the written Word of God. We must understand and embrace the fact that prophecy is not meant to release us from following the written Word of God, mature Godly counsel, and the Holy Spirit that dwells within us all. If we use prophecy as a convenient escape from pressure or correction, then obviously the intent of the prophetic word has been corrupted.

The Bible never states: "That as many that are led by the prophetic word, they are the sons of God." It is obedience first to the written Word of God that will bring our lives into Biblical order and divine fruitfulness. The prophetic word never allows us to violate clear Biblical principles laid down in Scripture, even if it did come with a "thus saith the Lord." Every word must be tried and proven before we act upon it.

The New Testament makes some very clear statements concerning prophecy. Let us examine a few of them.

1. Prophecy Must be Judged

I Corinthians 14:29. (KJV) Let the prophets speak two or three, and let the other judge.

(NIV) Two or three prophets should speak, and the others should weigh carefully what is said.

The Greek word translated "judge" in this passage means "to separate, to make a distinction, to discriminate or discern." The very fact that we are commanded by Scripture to discern or discriminate the word of prophecy speaks of its limitation. What does it mean to judge the prophetic word? How does one do this without becoming critical of the words which are anointed by the Holy Spirit and are truly what the Bible calls prophecy?

When prophecy comes forth in the corporate gathering of God's people, it should accomplish its Biblical purpose. The Apostle Paul gives several characteristics of true prophecy in I Corinthians 14:3 —

(KJV) — But he that prophesieth speaketh unto men to *edification*, and *exhortation*, and *comfort*.

(NIV) — But everyone who prophesies speaks to men for their *strengthening, encouragement* and *comfort*.

• Prophecy Should *Edify* the People of God.

The Greek work for edify is *olkodomeo*, which means "to be a housebuilder, to construct or build up, to confirm and strengthen." When prophecy is brought forth in the church service, we must ask ourselves, Is this constructive? Is this word building the House of God? Or destroying?

I Corinthians 14:12. Even so ye, forasmuch as ye are zealous of spiritual gifts, seek that ye may *excel* to the *edifying* of the church.

I Corinthians 14:4. . . . but he that prophesieth edifieth the church.

Prophecy is the spiritual gift which brings the greatest benefit to the Church. The ministry of the true anointed word of prophecy excels in strengthening the people of God.

When a person is first beginning to prophesy, he needs to be mindful his pride does not well up in the delusion that he is God's gift to the church for guidance and correction. I remember a certain occasion in a church service where a young man prophesied with great boldness, "Thus saith the Lord, ye stiff-necked, rebellious people, the Lord is here to rebuke and set in order. If you will not respond, the earth will open up and swallow you as He did with Korah!" Needless to say, the earth did not open up and the people did not respond to such harshness.

- Prophecy Should Give *Exhortation* to the People of God.

The Greek word translated "exhortation" is *parakleis*, whose root word is *parakalo*. This word has the meaning of calling someone to your side for the purpose of consoling, strengthening, and motivating. True prophecy is to provoke believers to good works, stirring them toward God and His love.

- Prophecy Should *Comfort* the People of God.

The Greek word for comfort is *paramuthia*; its root word being *paramutheomai*, meaning "to relate near so as to encourage someone who is weary, under pressure or afflictions." Prophecy will lift up the heads and hands that hang down in discouragement and will revive the wavering believer ready to give up the good fight of faith. True prophecy will bring a second wind to the runner lagging behind and cause him to finish the race.

- Prophecy Should Not Bring Confusion to God's People.

I Corinthians 14:33. For God is not the author of confusion, but of peace, as in all churches of the saints.

Paul clearly states that God does not initiate confusion in His people. The Holy Spirit brings peace to our hearts, not confusion. If the prophetic word robs us of our peace and leaves us in a state of uneasiness and confusion, then we should carefully discern who initiated this prophecy.

2. Prophecy Must be Proven

I Thessalonians 5:20-21. Despise not prophesyings. Prove all things; hold fast that which is good. (AMP) But test and prove all things until you can recognize what is good; to that hold fast.

The Apostle Paul exhorts us not to despise the word of prophecy. The NIV translation says it best: "Do not put out the Spirit's fire; do not treat prophecies with contempt." We are to respond to the prophetic word with respect and expectation.

At the same time Paul goes on to say we are to *prove* all things, hold fast to what is good. This is the unique balance of receiving the prophetic words, *caution* with *anticipation.*

The Greek word translated "prove" means "to examine, to put to the test, to recognize the genuine after examining closely." Prophecy must be put to the test in order to find the good, the genuine, the profitable. We are to eat the meat and spit out the bones. This is not optional but necessary for balanced Christian growth. The believer may prove the word of prophecy by asking the following questions:

Does this word contradict the written Word of God?

Does this word contradict the character attributes of God?

Does this word bear witness with my spirit?

Does this word have two or three confirmations? (Out of the mouth of two or three witnesses let every word be established.)

Does this word come forth from an established ministry that has a proven lifestyle and good fruit following his ministry?

10

Proper Perspective Toward Personal Prophecy

I Thessalonians 5:19-20. Quench not the Spirit. Despise not prophesyings.

The prophetic predictions found in Scripture are destined to happen; man has no control or influence in these prophecies. These prophetic words could be termed *fixed* prophecies. They are unchanging, sure, steadfast, accurate, and will happen exactly the way they are predicted in Scripture. Second Peter 1:19 reads, "We have also a more sure word of prophecy . . ."

The prophecy of Scripture is an unchanging word from God: you can live by it, die by it, make your decisions, raise your family, invest your money, and choose your friends by it, all with complete confidence. The prophecy of Scripture is absolutely trustworthy!

Matthew 5:18. For verily I say unto you, Till heaven and earth pass, one jot or one tittle shall in no wise pass from the law, till all be fulfilled.

Psalm 111:7. The works of his hands are verity and judgment; all his commandments are *sure*.

I Kings 8:56. Blessed be the Lord, that hath given rest unto His people Israel, according to all that he promised: there hath *not failed one word* of all his good promise, which he promised by the hand of Moses his servant.

Ezekiel 12:25. For I am the Lord: I will speak, and the word that I shall speak *shall come to pass*; it shall be no more prolonged: for in your days, O rebellious house, will I say the word, and *will perform* it, saith the Lord God.

The sure word of prophecy found in the Holy Scriptures is not to be doubted: it always accomplishes its purposes. Man may respond or react, believe or doubt, but he cannot influence the course of the prophecy of Scripture. These fixed prophecies are not contingent upon man's obedience or involvement; God will bring to pass every word because He is God. The responsibility of every believer toward the sure word of prophecy is to eagerly pray, watch, and expect God to work everything out according to His divine will.

Another realm of prophetic prediction that is of utmost importance to all believers is the realm of *personal prophecy*. While the prophecy of Scripture is unchangeable, sure, and worthy of all trust and confidence, personal prophecy is quite different. Personal prophecy is not fixed prophecy, destined to be fulfilled without help from anyone. Personal prophecy is that prophecy which a believer may receive from a qualified prophet or from a prophecy given in a church service by another believer.

Upon receiving a personal prophecy, the believer has certain God-given responsibilities that must be adhered to. The receiver of this type of prophecy has the responsibility for the prophecy's success or failure in its fulfillment. We may respond in obedience or react in carnal rebellion. We may believe and embrace the words as being from God and of necessity must be obeyed, or by human reasoning we may permit ourselves to obey the dictates of our own hearts. Whatever the case, the decision to respond lies in the hands of each believer. Just because a prophecy is received does not mean it will come to pass.

In order for personal prophecy to be fulfilled, the believer must act upon the words. He must obey its direct commands, prepare for the future ministries predicted, and adjust his lifestyle to respond on a daily basis to the word.

God works with man to bring the prophetic words to

pass, but He never violates man's free will. God will not bypass the fact that man must respond and move in faith toward obedience. The believer cannot approach personal prophecy in the same manner as the prophecy of Scripture.

I do not want to belittle the power of personal prophecy but rather to bring it into proper Biblical perspective. Over the years I have met with many believers to discuss their personal prophecies at length. During these conversations, many erroneous attitudes held by Christians toward personal prophecy have surfaced, sometimes accompanied by uneasiness, disappointment, and even irritation.

These mistaken attitudes may arise from ignorance because of lack of teaching, or because of the environment the believer has been spiritually nurtured in and influenced by. Such ignorance is ultimately molded into a particular belief or attitude. We must carefully examine ourselves in order to discern what attitudes we have cultivated toward prophecy and where they have originated. Let us list several of the common *errors* believers may fall into or grow into.

1. The error of *Taking No Responsibility* toward clear, direct promises in the personal prophecy. This attitude leans heavily on the sovereignty of God and does harm to human responsibility. (Acts 11:27-30; 13:1-4)

2. The error of *Total Dependence* upon the personal prophecies a person has received. The believer does not remain open to Godly counsel, or even to his common sense to help him make ordinary, mundane decisions. The believer begins to use his personal prophecy as if it were Scripture. The Bible clearly gives sound principles to live by, to make decisions by, and to grow unto maturity with. These principles cannot be broken to fulfill personal prophecy. The Scriptures never command us to totally depend upon the personal prophetic word we have received. This violates clear Biblical concepts and will lead

a person into self-deception.

Some Christians do not like to take responsibility for their actions or decisions, to the extreme of totally depending upon their prophecies for guidance. This is not only a form of escapism, this is turning our back on the opportunities God gives us to develop into mature Christians.

3. The error of *Humanistic-fatalism*. What will happen, will happen — I cannot change it! This attitude toward personal prophecy is more subtle than most attitudes. To some it is the ultimate faith confession. This error is accepted by both believers and non-believers alike and ultimately results in confusion, lethargy, lack of realism, lack of direction, and lack of clear vision of personal goals. If the prophetic word does not clearly state that you are to become a school teacher or an engineer, you could not assume that this was not to be your destiny, nor could you become fatalistic about your future. How could a personal prophecy cover the entire panorama of one's life? God still leads us by many ways — by His Holy Spirit, by Godly counsel, and by giving us ambitions.

11

The Believer's Responsibility to the Prophetic Word

Now that we have examined some of the improper responses a believer may have to personal prophecy, let us turn to the true Biblical responsibilities a believer must have to the prophetic word.

The prophetic word could be likened to a seed that must fall to the ground and then bring forth fruit. The analogy of the Word of God being likened to the seed is taught throughout the Scriptures. The Lord Jesus Christ teaches the same analogy in the parable of the sower in Matthew 13.

Let us look at the all important matter of the believer receiving a prophetic word into the good ground of his inner heart. In Matthew 13:3-23, Jesus speaks of the four *attitudes of the heart* which are represented by the four kinds of soil the seed could fall upon. Believers will respond to a prophetic word with the same four heart attitudes.

The first kind of soil speaks of the *heart which is not given to cultivate the Word of God in the midst of the busy routines of life.*

Matthew 13:19. When any one heareth the word of the kingdom, and understandeth it not, then cometh the wicked one, and catcheth away that which was sown in his heart. This is he which received seed by the way side.

The wayside was the path alongside the roads and highways between cities, the roads used in everyday life. A seed falling on this ground would lie on top of the earth, not being able to sprout as a seed that had fallen on farming ground. The seed does not penetrate the person's understanding because he is given to the natural mind, to the ways of the world. He is not seeking after God's Word or bringing God into the routine of his daily life. It is not that he has a major deterrent in his life to the ways of God; he simply has no desire or time to follow the Lord.

The second kind of soil speaks of the *hard heart which has no roots of Christlike character.*

Matthew 13:20-21 (NAS). "And the one on whom seed was sown on the rocky places, this is the man who hears the word, and immediately receives it with joy; yet he has no firm root in himself, but is only temporary, and when affliction or persecution arises because of the word, immediately he falls away."

In this type of soil the Word takes root but because the ground is stony — loose and gravelly, the roots can't take hold and form a strong root structure. The believer receives the Word with initial enthusiasm and joy, and it begins to grow within him. But when trials come he is easily swayed and the Word is uprooted.

These two verses contain two very important principles in receiving a word from the Lord. First of all, people receiving a prophetic word must understand that its fulfillment depends as much on the power of the prophetic word received as it does on the heart condition of the receiver. If we have no character roots and no depth of integrity, if our hearts are hard and shallow, then the word sowed into our lives will dwell within us only temporarily.

A hard heart will not allow a person to become rooted in the Word. He will only allow the Word to touch the areas of his personality which he permits. The Word is obstructed by not giving the Lord free course through his being.

The second important principle brought out by Jesus in verse 21 is that when affliction and persecution arise because of the Word, immediately the Word can fall away. Whenever we receive a word from the Lord, we receive the potential for that word to be tested and tried, and therefore affliction and persecution will arise in our lives. If we have no roots in ourselves or strength to wage a good warfare with the word received, in times of affliction and persecution the word will immediately fall away from us. We will be as one who never received that word.

Therefore the sayings of Jesus are important to those who receive prophetic words. We must cultivate a heart that has character and strength that can retain the good words the Lord would sow among us.

The third kind of soil is the heart attitude of *incomplete surrender to the Lordship of Jesus Christ.*

Matthew 13:22 (NAS). "And the one on whom seed was sown among the thorns, this is the man who hears the word, and the worry of the world, and the deceitfulness of riches choke the word, and it becomes unfruitful."

There is nothing wrong with the seed — the seed is incorruptible good and comes from God. But if the soil is not cultivated, it cannot bring forth the seed.

Hearts must be prepared and cultivated so that the word received from God will not be choked out or stunted in its growth. When the spirit of this world has not been weeded out of our heart ground, the thorns of deceitfulness and materialism, the thorns of anxiety and worry will choke out the prophetic word and it cannot produce fruit.

There is nothing wrong with the prophetic word that has been sown into the man's life. The problem is that he did not tear down and destroy the thorns and the thistles that were dwelling within his heart to make room for the good word of God to bring forth fruit. He has not taken consideration to remove from his life those things which compete against the word of God.

The Word of God should have complete reign in our lives. "Seek ye first the kingdom of God, and His righteousness; and all these things shall be added unto you" (Matthew 6:33). If one has rooted out the thorns and thistles and has put God first, there is nothing wrong with the riches which come as a natural outgrowth of God being within us.

The fourth kind of soil is the *good heart that understands the Word.*

Matthew 13:23 (NAS). "And the one on whom seed was sown on the good ground, this is the man who hears the word and understands it; who indeed bears fruit, and brings forth, some a hundredfold, some sixty, and some thirty."

The fourth kind of soil that the Word of the Lord will fall upon is the soil of a good and honest heart. The word "honest" in Greek means "sound or healthy, praiseworthy, pure without hypocrisy or pretension." The good soil is the honest heart of a man who can hear the Word of God and understand it. When we cultivate such a heart attitude of honesty and integrity, we will receive the seed of the Word of God and it will bring forth fruit every time without error.

With this understanding of the four heart attitudes, let us read Luke's account of the parable of the sower.

Luke 8:4-8 (NAS). And when a great multitude were coming together, and those from the various cities were journeying to Him, He spoke by way of a parable:

"The sower went out to sow his seed; and as he sowed, some fell beside the road; and it was trampled under foot, and the birds of the air devoured it.

"And other seed fell on rocky soil, and as soon as it grew up, it withered away, because it had no moisture.

"And other seed fell among the thorns; and the thorns grew up with it, and choked it out.

"And other seed fell into the good ground, and grew up, and produced a crop a hundred times as great." As He said these things, He would call out, "He who has ears to hear, let him hear."

The Book of James adds another thought about the kind of heart we should have when we receive the word of the Lord.

James 1:17-25 (NAS). Every good thing bestowed and every perfect gift is from above, coming down from the Father of lights, with whom there is no variation, or shifting shadow.

In the exercise of His will He brought us forth by the word of truth, so that we might be, as it were, the first fruits among His creatures.

This you know, my beloved brethren. But let every one be quick to hear, slow to speak and slow to anger;

for the anger of man does not achieve the righteousness of God.

Therefore putting aside all filthiness and all that remains of wickedness, in humility receive the word implanted, which is able to save your souls.

But prove yourselves doers of the word, and not merely hearers who delude themselves.

For if any one is a hearer of the word and not a doer, he is like a man who looks at his natural face in a mirror;

for once he has looked at himself and gone away, he has immediately forgotten what kind of person he was.

But one who looks intently at the perfect law, the law of liberty, and abides by it, not having become a forgetful hearer but an effectual doer, this man shall be blessed in what he does.

In these verses, the Apostle James gives us the account of a man receiving a good word from the Lord. In verse 17, James says that every gift bestowed upon us comes from above, from the Father of lights. When we receive a prophetic word from the Lord, it is a good gift coming forth from the Father, who can only give what is good. In verse 21, James says that by receiving the word with meekness and humility, it will be able to change us and even to save us from great destruction and disaster.

Let us also turn to I Thessalonians 2:13 where Paul teaches another important principle in receiving the word of the Lord. "For this cause also thank we God without ceasing, because, when ye received the word of God which ye heard of us, ye received it not as the word of men, but as it is in truth, the word of God which effectually worketh also in you that believe."

In this verse Paul gives us a very important principle. We are to accept the prophetic word, not as the word of men, but as the word of God which is able to work in us and perform in us the good will of the Father.

The Apostle Paul also adds another Scripture to the way a believer should receive a word in his Epistle to the Hebrews 2:1. "Therefore we ought to give the more earnest heed to the things which we have heard, lest at any time we should let them slip." Paul here speaks about giving heed to the word we have received. The word "heed" in Greek means "to lean forward and pay very close attention so as to let nothing slip away, that nothing be wasted." When we receive a word from the Lord, we must pay very close attention with our spiritual hearts and ears. Many times believers receive a word with such haphazardness and superficiality that the word is soon lost — just because they were not paying close attention to what the Lord said.

We need to treat these words with great sensitivity and responsibility. When the word is given to us we become the stewards of the word of God. We will have to answer to the Lord for what we have done with all the prophetic words and the quickened words that have come to us by the Holy Spirit.

All of the attitudes we have examined are very important for growing in and maturing by the·prophetic words given to us by the Lord. We must receive the word of God with a good and honest heart, with humility and meekness, with careful attentiveness, and finally, as a word of God, not of man. If we receive the prophetic word with these attitudes, the word will always become fruitful in our lives and move us on toward perfection.

Another area to be examined is the testing of the word that comes into our life. There is a divine principle found throughout Scripture concerning prophetic words: the word is received, the word is tested, and then the word is fulfilled. Many Christians would like to receive a dynamic word, bypass this middle stage of the testing of the word, and enter into that word without any persecution.

Nevertheless, the Bible does not teach this, nor do the experiences of Godly people throughout history and in the present day. Whenever the Lord puts forth a word, whether it is a Biblical Word, a command, a promise, or a prophetic word received into our lives as a promise, that word will be tested and tried, and it will come to pass as we respond to the test.

In the Gospel of John 10:10, the Lord Jesus teaches us the nature of the enemy that attacks us and the purpose of his attack. "The thief cometh not, but for to steal, and to kill, and to destroy: I am come that they might have life, and that they might have it more abundantly." When we receive a word from the Lord, immediately the thief will come to try to steal the blessing and the promise that the Lord has given us. The devil is a thief and has been a thief from the beginning. He comes to steal anything he can pressure out of our lives, or that he can get us to throw away and say is not really from the Lord.

The dictionary defines the word "thief" as "one who takes the goods or personal property of another without his knowledge or consent, without any intention of returning." The devil truly is a thief and he will come and take all spiritual properties and spiritual knowledge from you without your consent if you do not protect the word that God gives you.

The enemy has many ways of stealing the word of God from us. Often he throws discouragement our way, blow by blow, time after time. As we become worn down, our faith weakens. Without diligently and fervently applying our faith to the word, the word will never come to pass.

He may come and rob the seed from our hearts before it has taken hold within our spirits, so that it never even develops.

He will throw confusion into our minds. Genesis 3 is an illustration of how the thief will come with confusion to steal the good word of God from our lives. Genesis 3:1 reads, "Now the serpent was more subtil than any beast of the field which the Lord God had made. And he said unto the woman, Yea, hath God said, Ye shall not eat of every tree of the garden?"

We must remember as believers that the serpent, or the devil, is a very crafty being. He will use any craftiness he can think of that could destroy our lives. He delights in confusing us by twisting the word God gave us so that we begin to question the word or begin to think maybe we misunderstood it. In verse 1, the devil says, "Yea, hath God said?" This is the way the thief keeps after us: "Has God said?" "Did God really say that?" "Are you sure that this is what the Lord is going to do?"

We must rebuke the devourer. We must close our ears to any twisting of the good word of God. We must not allow the thief to steal what God has given us to bring forth great things.

In Luke 8:15, we read that we should hear the Word, retain it, and by persevering, produce a good crop. When the prophetic word comes into our lives, we must hear it — pay close attention to what the Lord is saying; retain it — make sure it is planted deep within our hearts; and then by persevering — by enduring — put our shoulders to the task. If we do these things we will produce a good crop. But if we let the thief come in and steal the seed, there will be no crop at all.

In Hebrews 6:12, the author declares that we should "be not slothful, but followers of them who through faith and patience inherit the promises." Here we have another very important principle in bringing the prophetic word to its complete fulfillment. The Apostle here gives us two key New Testament words which must be acted upon in our lives. The qualities of "faith" and "patience" are prerequisites to inheriting the promise.

Whenever the prophetic word comes to us, we must adhere to that word with faith. Hebrews 4:2 says, "For unto us was the Gospel preached, as well as unto them: but the word preached did not profit them, not being mixed with faith in them that heard it." When we receive a word from God, that word must be united with faith in order for that word to profit us and to come to pass in our lives. There have been many instances of people receiving a prophetic word from the Lord, but who stumbled in disbelief or through their own narrowness of mind and smallness of heart. They have canceled the great promises of God.

The Bible says we are to unite the word with faith, and then with patience wait for that word to come to pass. When God spoke unto Abraham and told him to sacrifice Isaac, his only son given to him by God through a miracle, it took a tremendous faith for Abraham to obey the word of God. It took great patience for Abraham to wait and see the hand of the Lord in his circumstance.

Whatever great mountain God has given us to climb, or whatever great Canaan land God has promised us for an inheritance, we, like Israel, and all the Old Testament characters, must by faith possess the inheritance of God, and do this through the work of patience. Whenever God gives a prophetic word, that word may take years to come to fulfillment. There may be many Jordans to cross, there may be many giants to kill, there may be many Canaan lands to inherit – sometimes it takes a long time to possess all the promises of the Lord.

Let us not become weary in well doing, let us not quit right before we come to the finish. Let us not say in our hearts, "How can God bring this to pass, for it is such a large promise?" If we unite these promises with faith, and endure through patience, we will see God bring to pass all the words that He has given us in years gone by.

Whenever we receive that good word from the Lord, we must understand that there will be a fight, a warfare in order to bring that word to fulfillment. The Apostle Paul knew this, and thus he exhorted his spiritual son Timothy to make certain he held on to the prophetic words that went over him and fought the good fight of faith. In I Timothy 1:18 we read, "This charge I commit unto thee, my son Timothy, according to the prophecies which went before on thee, that thou by them mightest war a good warfare; holding faith and a good conscience; which some having put away concerning faith have made shipwreck."

We as believers must take all the prophecies that have gone over us and with them wage a mighty warfare of faith and patience to bring them to pass. Let us not be negligent, let us not be slothful in enduring the afflictions and the trials that might come into our lives because of the word. Let us not be shallow, or let the thorns of our heart choke out the mighty promises of God. For it takes faith, it takes willingness to see the word of the Lord come to pass.

Whenever we enter into this race, and into the arena of faith, we must begin to pace ourselves, and understand we are in a race for life. We are not just in a short sprint, we are in a long marathon that will have many obstacles and many challenges. Yet there is a crown of life and a crown of joy for all those who finish the race that God has given to them.

We must not strive in ourselves to fulfill any word the Lord has given us. We must not engage in any kind of a struggle with the Lord to bring the word of the Lord to pass. If God has spoken it, nothing will keep it from coming to pass. If God has said it, there are not enough devils in hell or enough darkness in the world to cause that word to be nullified. When God says something, it will surely come to pass. We do not have to try to help the Lord out, or try to give the Lord ideas of what to do to help that word. We must simply move in faith and have the good patience that the Lord gives us to bring that word to pass.

In Genesis 16 we read the story about Abraham and Sarah beginning to doubt and strive with the word of the Lord. Out of their doubt and impatience came forth their own idea of how to bring about the miracle in their lives. We know the story of how Sarah suggested to Abraham to go in unto her maid-servant Hagar, and through Hagar God would raise up the seed that was promised. Hagar was not the will of the Lord, and He rejected the seed that came through her. Abraham and Sarah still had to wait many years before God gave them the miracle birth and the miracle seed in Isaac.

We must let God work out His Word and have that faith of God and that patience of God that knows unshakeably that the Lord God will bring to pass every word He has spoken.

~ ~ ~

City Bible Publishing
Training Resources

Seasons of Intercession
Frank Damazio

Seasons of Intercession reveals God's desire for prayer-intercession for every believer's life and demonstrates prayer strategies that will change lives, empower churches and shape futures.
ISBN 1-886849-08-0 HC
ISBN 1-886849-11-0 SC

Seasons of Revival
Frank Damazio

Seasons of Revival offers fresh insight in understanding God's seasons of outpouring. The truths presented in this book will enable you to enjoy greater refreshing during this season of revival.
ISBN 1-886849-04-8

From Barrenness to Fruitfulness
Frank Damazio

This book draws a parallel between biological barrenness and the barrenness that often occurs in churches and ministries. Frank Damazio uses his own testimony-and those of biblical characters who struggled with barrenness-to provide comfort and instruction for people suffering through seasons of unfruitfulness in ministry.
ISBN 0-8307-2337-4

Vanguard Leader
Frank Damazio

Vanguard Leader defines the characteristics, function and motivation of true leadership. It addresses the major issues facing the church in this era.
ISBN 0-914936-53-0

The Making of a Leader
Frank Damazio

This bestseller presents a scriptural analysis of the philosophy, history, qualifications and practice of Christian leadership. You will be challenged by the illustrations from the life of David and others.
ISBN 0-914936-84-0

Timothy Training Program
Frank Damazio

How does a pastor keep up with all the demands of building a church? The *Timothy Training Program* will provide the tools for training new leaders.

Teachers ISBN 0-914936-12-3
Students ISBN 0-914936-13-1

Ask for these resources at your local Christian bookstore.

City Bible Publishing
www.citybiblepublishing.com
equip@citybiblepublishing.com

9200 NE Fremont, Portland, OR 97220 USA
Phone: (503) 253-9020 ● (800) 777-6057 ● Fax: (503) 257-2228
City Bible Publishing is a ministry of
City Bible Church (formerly Bible Temple) in Portland, Oregon, USA.